Gifted to:

From:

Something Amazing

I dedicate this work of art to my family and friends.
You are all Something Amazing.
Thank you Mother Ocean for being my most respected muse and
teaching me so much.
Thank you: Mimi & Papa for showing me the meaning of True Love, Mom for
teaching me that friendships are Something Amazing, Pop for showing me
persistence and determination alone are omnipotent
and brother for being my brother.
I love you all.

SOMETHING AMAZING
© 2015 Steven C. Fawley
Second Edition

All rights reserved.
Printed and bound in China through Asia Pacific Offset

Written and Designed by Steve Fawley

Something Amazing was hand illustrated in Bali
by Nyoman Santosa in traditional Batuan style.
Pencil, pen, ink wash & watercolor.

www.somethingamazingbook.com

Library of Congress Control Number 2015907435

ISBN 978-0-615-46121-2

Something Amazing

By

Steve Fawley

2015

Illustrated

By

NyomanART

There once was a snail
who lived in a shell.
Alone on the beach
she would play.

Through sunny days
and *foggy* haze,
she would play,
she would play,
she would play.

The wind blew by.
A seagull cried.
Alone on the beach
She would play.

One day at play
near her favorite bay
sitting up on Jump Rock
she got a big SHOCK !!!

So she climbed up a tree
to see what it might be.
Looking out at the ocean
a strange commotion...

Having never seen such a sight
under the yellow sunlight.
She stayed up in the tree
and thought what could it be?

What could it be
that strange commotion?
What could it be
out there in the ocean?

Time went by.
The tide got high
but no reply.

Far, far from the land,
a distant shape that
looked like a hand?
A hand!
That far from the land!!
Impossible, she thought.
Then there it was again.

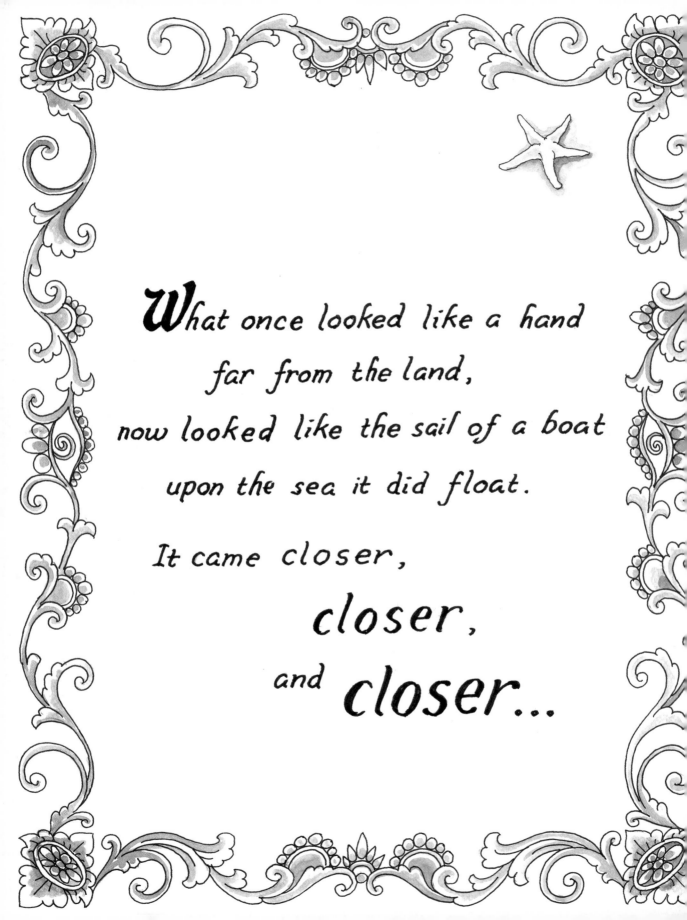

What once looked like a hand
far from the land,
now looked like the sail of a boat
upon the sea it did float.

It came closer,

closer,

and closer...

The snail soon saw
that it was not a hand
far from the land,
nor was it the sail of a boat
upon the sea it did float.

To her surprise
she realized
it was a tail.

A GREAT BLUE WHALE !!!

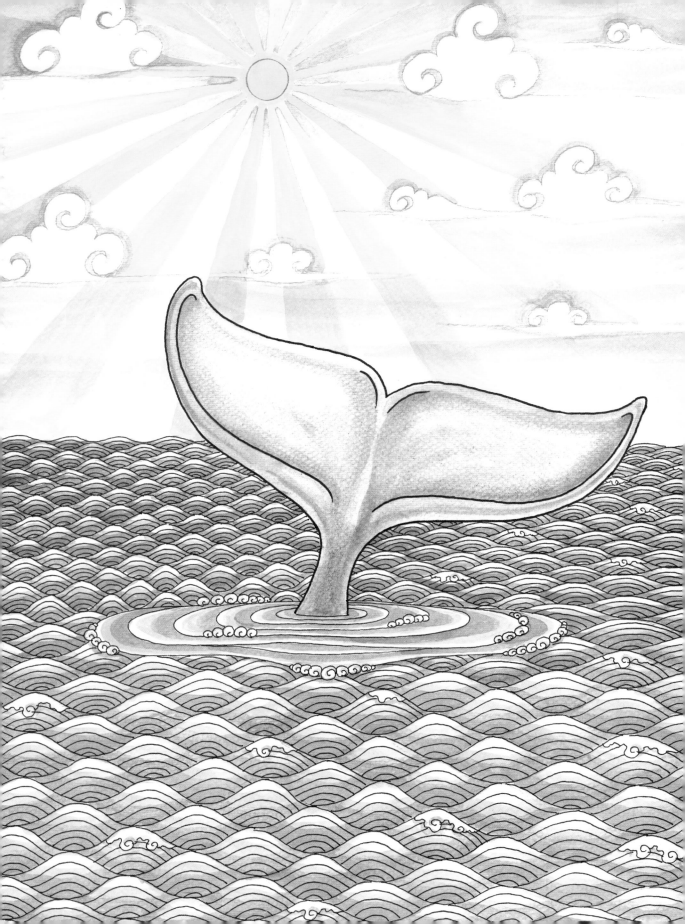

Excited to meet this
whale with the tail
she climbed down from the tree
and shouted out,

"O please!
O please!
O please be nice to me!
You could eat me like a fish
but that would not be my wish.
I am looking for a friend,
not for my life to end."

"A friend indeed
    you will find in me."
As the whale laughed to the sky
    and gave his reply,
"My new found friend
    your life will not end.
        I was alone today
            when I saw you at play.
        So I swam in this bay
            with these words to say:
If you want to go play
    then come my way.
        Adventure awaits us
            somewhere far, far away."

An adventure sounds fun
under the sun
She thought for a moment,
for two,
and then three.

"That's it !
That's it !!
Surfing !!!
Surfing !!!

I want to go surfing
and ride the wild blue waves."

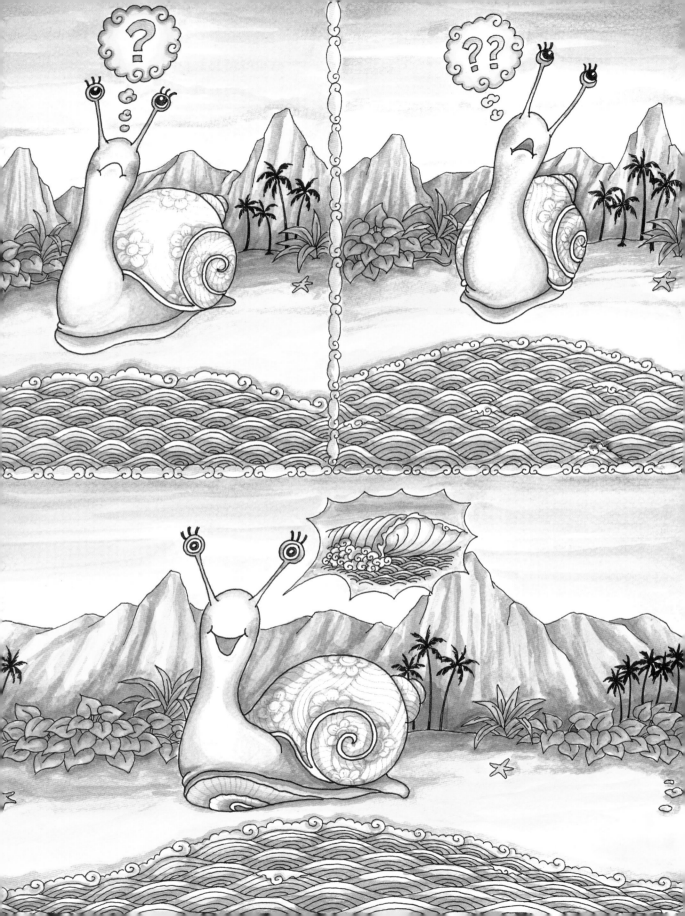

"But I have not a boat
and my shell will not float!
What can I do?
Go surfing with you?"

"Yes, with me.
Come surfing with me.
I can show you the way
across from this bay
there's a magical wave."

"Yes please!
O please,
please take me away.
I must catch a wave!"

So he let down his tail
soon to set sail.
She climbed up his tail
and on to his back
then sat with a smile
now seeing for miles.

They traveled the sea
into the day
across the bay
to the magical wave.

They got Closer,
Closer,
and Closer!!!

As they approached the wave

the snail sat in a daze -

such perfect waves !!!

"Alive we ride!
Let's flow with the tide.
Safe on my back
I will show you an
off the lip WHACK!!!"

A cut back

with a **SMACK !!!**

Get a barrel
or two !!!

And surf with
the Cosmic Dolphins too!!!

From atop the whale, the snail
had the most wonderful experience.
Surfing was like nothing
she had ever done before.
But soon came the time
when they had to travel
back through that day,
now so far away.

Back through the day
and into the night
when they finally got home,
such sweet dreams delight.

He then lowered her down
back to the ground.
She looked up into his eyes
and said,
"Thank you my friend!
Thank you for everything.
Thank you for all!!
Thank you for
taking me surfing...!!! "

With loving laughs out loud,

blue moon and a cloud,

rain drops from the sky

and in saying good-bye

they both agreed their friendship

is

Something
Amazing!!!

They then turned their heads
with hopes for their beds.
To dream of the fun
they had under the sun
and knowing,
just knowing . . .

*Their love would
one day meet again...*

And again . . .

And again.

The
End